Clever Kids

Science
Ages 8-10

World Book, Inc.

Chicago London Sydney Toronto

Kids: The answer key is on page 32.

World Book, Inc.
525 W. Monroe
Chicago, IL 60661

For information on other World Book products, call 1-800-255-1750.

ISBN: 0-7166-9206-6
LC: 95-61314

Printed in Mexico

2 3 4 5 6 7 8 9 10 99 98 97 96 95

Contents

What Makes Science Scientific?

★ What causes a rainbow?
★ Can plants grow in the dark?
★ Why does tightening a guitar string make it sound a higher note?

Have you ever asked questions like these about things around you? One way to get answers is to ask someone. But suppose the person you ask doesn't know. You might try looking in books for information. But what do you do if you can't find the answer to your question? You might give up. Or you might take steps to find out for yourself. That's what a scientist does. Following are some methods and materials scientists and others use to find answers to their questions.

Observing and recording

Sometimes you can find an answer to your question just by observing an event and keeping a record of what happens. For example, scientists easily can observe how chimpanzees behave by going to a zoo. Some scientists, such as zoologist (zoh AHL uh jihst) Jane Goodall, travel to observe chimpanzees and other animals in their natural surroundings.

Analyzing data and discovering connections

However, what you observe doesn't always make sense right away. In these cases, you might decide it is better to compare and contrast different data, or bits of information, looking for connections that help explain why

things are as they are. For example, you may wonder why oaks, maples, and many other kinds of trees lose their leaves in winter, while pine trees keep theirs. Then you may observe that pine leaves are needle-shaped, while the leaves of other trees are flat. Your observations may lead you to believe there is a connection between the shape of a tree's leaves and whether the tree loses its leaves in winter.

Making a hypothesis and testing it

In still other cases, you can't always observe clearly the event you have questions about. It might have happened too long ago or too far away. Maybe it takes place too quickly or too slowly. Perhaps what is changing is far too huge

or tiny to be seen. In such cases, you need to make an intelligent guess—called a *hypothesis* (hy PAH thuh sihs)—and then perform tests to discover whether you guessed correctly. In the example of the leaves above, you may form a hypothesis that needle-shaped leaves withstand cold better than flat leaves. To test it, you might collect many different types of leaves and put them in the freezer, then see how they look when you thaw them out. Tracking down an answer in this way is what scientists call using scientific method, which consists of five steps.

The scientific method

1. Define the problem. Identify one question you want to answer.

2. Come up with a possible answer, a hypothesis, to your question.

3. Create an experiment that will test your hypothesis. Choose the materials and methods to use in the experiment. Plan to work the experiment more than once, changing only the ingredient or process being tested.

4. Perform the test and collect the data: Observe, measure, and record all the information in a log or notebook. Repeat the experiment as needed.

5. Draw a conclusion based on the data. If the conclusion doesn't agree with your hypothesis, develop a new hypothesis to test.

Keeping a science notebook

A good scientist always takes notes. To be ready at all times to record your scientific observations and thoughts, keep a notebook handy. Yours can be a loose-leaf binder, a spiral notepad, a hard-cover blank book, or whatever works best for you. When you write or draw in your science notebook, be sure to record the date and time. Throughout the activities in this book, you will be asked to make predictions and drawings and to record data in your log. But use it whenever you like to record other questions, thoughts, and information.

Assembling a science kit

You can find the supplies you need for these activities around the house or get them at a store. But it might be fun to put together your own science kit, so it will be handy whenever you want to do an experiment. Here are a few items you may want to include:

- ★ Thermometer
- ★ Magnifying glass
- ★ Balloons
- ★ Ruler or tape measure
- ★ Small scale
- ★ Spoons for stirring and measuring
- ★ Glass or plastic jars, bottles, or other containers
- ★ Tape
- ★ Funnel
- ★ Cloth for wiping spills
- ★ Safety glasses
- ★ Pens or pencils
- ★ Medicine dropper
- ★ Rubber bands

These are only suggestions. Your science kit may have many very different items, depending on what you're interested in.

Getting started

In this book, we have used several abbreviations. Here is a list of them, along with their meanings:

cm	centimeter
ft	foot
in	inch
ml	milliliter
oz	ounce
Tbs	tablespoon

When you see the symbol ⚠ it means that you should be extra careful when doing the activity, and get a grown-up to help you.

Science is constantly changing. Scientists keep looking for more information and better explanations for what they find. The activities and experiments in this book will get you started on your way to join all the others who are curious about the world around us. The results of an activity may lead you to ask more questions. If so, good! Keep asking questions, and then find answers to them.

Nature Up Close

YOU NEED:
★ A slice of fresh bread ★ A plastic bag ★ A magnifying glass (An inexpensive one will do nicely.) ★ A pencil ★ Paper ★ Fish scales ★ A mirror

Did you ever see a picture of a detective? Illustrators often show make-believe detectives peering through magnifying glasses, looking for clues so small that they would be overlooked by most people. Magnifying glasses can help you, too—when you want to see tiny things better than by using your eyes alone.

It is interesting to see little organisms called fungi (FUHN jy) up close. But before you can study real live fungi, you have to grow them. Here's an easy way to do it. Before you start, maybe you'd like to make a sketch of what you think the fungi will look like magnified. Use your imagination!

1. Seal a slice of moist bread in a plastic bag and set it in a warm place.

2. After a few days, you should have a nice crop of fungi. Look at them with the magnifying glass. Can you see how fuzzy they look? Can you see where the fungi are reaching out to form new fungi? What colors do you see?

Try to grow fungi on other kinds of moist food. Are all the fungi the same? How are they different? Record your findings.

Even your own body is fascinating under a magnifying glass. Try a few of these and draw pictures of what you see:

★ Look at fingernail clippings. Are they similar in any way to fish scales? Do you see layers in them?

★ Look at hairs from your head. Can you see different thicknesses? Compare your hair with hairs from a cat or dog. How are they different?

★ What does your tongue look like, up close? Use a mirror to see inside your mouth. Do you see your taste buds? Are they all the same or are some bigger than others?

★ Look at your fingerprints. Do all your fingers have the same pattern? In what ways are your fingerprints different from a friend's fingerprints?

Another item that is interesting under a magnifying glass is fish scales. You can get some at a grocery store. Rinse them and look at them through the magnifier. Then separate one scale from the rest. Under the magnifying glass, you will see tiny circular lines. Every year, one darker line forms, so if you count these, it will tell you how old the fish is. It's like counting rings to find out how old a tree is. But with fish, the newest lines are on the inside and the oldest are on the outer edges of the scale. Are some of the rings narrower or farther apart? What might this tell you about the fish's growth rate?

What Plants Need

YOU NEED:
- ★ One of these materials: cotton balls, paper towels, tissues, sand, kitty litter, or gravel
- ★ Seven seed containers made of plastic or some other nonporous material
- ★ Grass seeds or radish seeds ★ Water ★ Plastic wrap

Plants are everywhere! From your own backyard or neighborhood park, to mountains, deserts, and even marshes and ponds, the world is blanketed with plants. What conditions are necessary for plant growth?

nonporous: having no pores (tiny holes) that things such as air or water can pass through.

Here's a list of words to think about: sunlight, water, air, shade, soil, warmth, food. Which of these do you think are most important for growing healthy plants?

Make the table below in your notebook and fill it in with your predictions about what would happen to a plant with too much or too little of the conditions listed. Then try the activity on page 11 to test your predictions.

	Too little	Too much
sunlight		
water		
air		
shade		
soil		
warmth		
food		

1. Choose one of the materials listed in the first entry of the *You Need* list to use in place of soil. Fill the seven containers approximately two-thirds full of the material.

2. Sprinkle a few seeds on top of each of the minigardens.

3. Take two of the minigardens. Place one container in a sunny spot and the other in a dark closet. Make sure you keep the plants equally moist.

4. Take two more of your containers. Tightly cover one of the containers with plastic wrap so it doesn't get any air. Put both these containers in a sunny spot.

5. Fill the first of the remaining three containers with so much water that you cover the seeds. Just moisten the seeds in the second container. Put no water in the last container. Put these three containers in a sunny spot.

6. Wait about a week. Then observe all the plants. Which place did the plants like better, the dark closet or the one with bright sunlight? Which seeds did better, the ones with air or those without? How did the different amounts of water affect the growth of the seeds? Record your observations.

7. Review your notes on all three groups. Make a list of desirable growing conditions for plants. Compare it with your predictions.

If you want to, you can vary your experiments in a number of ways. For example, you can test conditions such as sunny with a lot of water, dark with a lot of water, and sunny with medium water. Or, you can continue the experiments by choosing healthy seedlings and adding different substances to the pots. You could try soaking eggshells in water for a few days and then water your seedlings with it. Or sprinkle ashes from a barbecue or fireplace in your pots. Do these substances affect your plants? If so, why? What other tests can you think of?

Up and Down and Side to Side

YOU NEED:

activity 1 ★ A glass jar ★ Four dried navy or lima beans ★ Paper towels or cotton balls

activity 2 ★ A shoebox ★ Two pieces of cardboard or tagboard ★ Scissors ★ Tape ★ A runner bean seed ★ A little clay pot or other small container ★ Potting soil

We've learned that all plants need water and light to thrive. But just how important are they? Here are two activities to show just how hard plants will work to get them.

But first . . .

Here are two new words to think about:

geotropism (jee AHT ruh pihz uhm)

phototropism (foh TAHT ruh pihz uhm)

Geo means *Earth,* and *photo* means *light.* The second part of both these words, *tropism,* means *turning.*

So what do these words mean, and what do they have to do with plants?

Activity 1: Rooting Roots

1. Soak about four dried beans in water overnight.

2. Stuff a glass jar full of paper towels or cotton balls and add enough water to wet them.

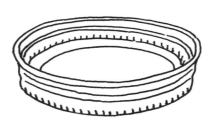

3. Place the beans between the towel and the glass jar, so you can see them. Place two of the beans with the little nub facing the top of the jar, one with the nub facing the bottom, and one with it facing the side. Leave the lid off the jar.

After a few days, the beans will sprout and begin to send out roots in search of water. The plant has used up most of the food that was stored in the bean, and now it needs to find a way to make more.

4. After several days, in which direction do the roots grow? Why does the bean search there to find water? Think about where water is usually found. But your beans are surrounded by water. Is it something else? Record your thoughts and observations.

5. Make sure the paper towel is moist and put the lid back on the jar. Turn the jar upside down and wait a few more days. In which direction are the roots growing now? How can you explain this? (Hint: remember the word *geotropism* on page 12!)

Activity 2: Plant Workout

How hard will plants work to get light? This experiment will suggest an answer.

1. Soak a runner bean seed in water overnight. Then plant it in a small container filled with moist potting soil.

2. Cut away one short end of a shoebox. Stand the shoebox so the open end is on top. Set the pot inside the box toward one side.

3. Cut the two cardboard cards so that they are the same size as the end of the shoebox.

4. About 1/2 in (1.25 cm) from one end of each card, cut a square "window" about 2 in by 2 in (5 cm by 5 cm). Tape one of the cards inside the shoebox to make a shelf above the pot. Position the window on the side of the box away from the pot. Now put the cover back on the box and wait a few days. Write or draw what you think will happen.

5. After the bean sprouts, check in what direction its stem grows. How do you explain the growth?

6. Now tape the other card about 2 in (5 cm) above the first card, this time with the window on the opposite side. Predict what will happen. In what direction does the stem grow after a few days? Collect your thoughts and conclusions in your journal.

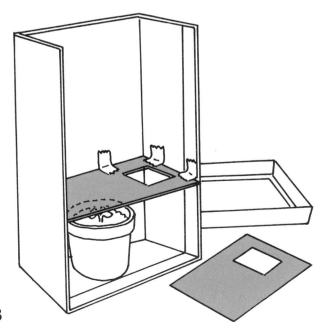

How Does Your Tongue Taste?

YOU NEED:
- ★ Four medicine droppers (You can use cotton swabs if no medicine droppers are available)
- ★ Four spoons ★ Four cups ★ Water ★ Salt ★ Sugar ★ Lemon juice ★ Instant coffee
- ★ One or more friends ★ A blindfold

Your senses link you to the world. They allow you to see, smell, hear, taste, and feel things in your environment. One of the senses that is the most fun is the sense of taste. Without taste, we could not tell if foods were salty, sweet, sour, or bitter. Chocolate pudding would taste the same as oatmeal. You might as well eat dry toast instead of pizza.

You know that you use your tongue to taste things. But did you know that different parts of your tongue seem to specialize in certain tastes? You can make a map of the parts of your tongue and the foods they taste best. Begin with the map of the tongue that you see on this page. Each part of the tongue tends to specialize in a particular taste. The four kinds of tastes are sweet, salty, bitter, and sour. Sugar is sweet, salt is salty, lemon juice is sour, and coffee is bitter. Where can you taste each one best?

1. Put about 4 oz (120 ml) of water in each cup. Add a spoonful of one of the flavorings to each cup and mix well.

2. Have a friend put on a blindfold and stick out his or her tongue. Squeeze or swab several drops of one of the solutions on your friend's tongue in one of the regions shown on the tongue map. Ask your friend to describe the taste (sweet, salty, sour, bitter). Record where you place the solution and your friend's response. Repeat the process for each of the other solutions, all in the same place on the tongue. Record the results.

3. Repeat *step 2* for each of the other areas of the tongue. Before you begin each new series of tests, let your friend rinse his or her mouth out with plain water.

4. After you have finished testing all the solutions on all your friends, study what you wrote down. Where do your friends taste sweet things best? Where do they taste salty things best? What about bitter or sour things?

Now think up some of your own experiments. For example, make the solutions weaker. Are some of your friends better at identifying tastes than others? Add sugar to the lemon so it's both sweet and sour. What areas of the tongue respond to that flavor? Does any single region register the true flavor? What about sweetened coffee, or salty lemon juice? Be creative!

You've Got Some Nerve(s)!

YOU NEED:
activity 1 ★ A 3-in-by-5-in (7.5-cm-by-12.5-cm) index card or other stiff card about that size ★ Two different colored crayons, markers, or colored pencils ★ A yardstick

activity 2 ★ Several index cards ★ A box of pins ★ A blindfold

What do you know about your senses? It's true that we feel with our skin, hear with our ears, and smell with our nose. But it's really the network of nerves linking all parts of our body to our brain that makes it possible for us to experience the world through our senses. The following two activities will show you a little about how important nerves are.

sensory: having to do with senses.

Activity 1: Finding Your Blind Spot

1. Near the edge of the index card or cardboard, draw a solid circle about 1/2 in (1.25 cm) in diameter. Near the opposite edge, draw an X in the other color.

2. Cover your left eye. Look at the circle as you pull the paper closer to your face. At one point, the X will vanish. Then you will see it again as you pull the card even closer. The point at which the X became invisible is your blind spot. Measure the distance from the card to your face. Record it.

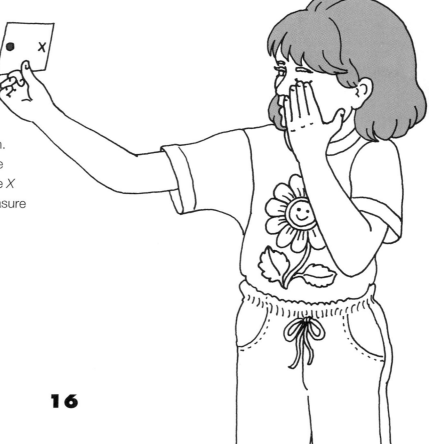

3. Now flip the card upside down and repeat *step 2* with your right eye closed. Does the blind spot for this eye appear at the same distance from your face?

Why do you think you can't see the *X* at one point? The inside layer of the eye, the *retina* (REH tih nuh), is made of nerve tissues that pick up light images and send them on to the brain along the optic nerve. At the place where the optic nerve connects with the eye, there are no nerve tissues. What do you think happens to images that fall on that spot? And why don't you normally notice the blind spot?

Activity 2: That's Touching

Is your skin's sense of touch the same all over your body? If your answer is no, write down a few guesses about where your skin is most sensitive. Compare the results of the following experiment to your prediction.

1. In one index card, stick at least three pins very close together. In another card, stick a few pins about 1-1/2 in (3.75 cm) apart. In the third card, insert the pins about 2-1/2 in (6.25 cm) apart. On all three cards, make sure the pin points are level.

2. Blindfold a friend. Gently touch the pinheads, each card in turn, to your friend's arm, leg, palm, scalp, lips, and then fingers. Ask your friend to tell how many pins he or she feels at each location with each card. Record the results. Where are your friend's guesses most accurate? Those are the places with many nerve endings placed close together.

Do-It-Yourself Erosion

YOU NEED:
activity 1 ★ A drinking straw ★ Modeling clay or chewed chewing gum
★ A glass of water ★ A freezer

activity 2 ★ A new bar of soap ★ A water faucet ★ A sensitive scale—
possibly a postage or food scale

Have you ever visited the Grand Canyon in Arizona or seen pictures of it? Have you ever held soil in your hand? Would you be surprised to learn that millions upon millions of years ago the Grand Canyon was a gently rolling plain? Or that your handful of soil was once rocks and living plants and animals? The forces of Earth—wind, water, and changing temperatures—shaped our planet into what it is today. The activities on these pages will help you see clearly how forces constantly change Earth.

erosion (ih ROH zhuhn): the wearing away of rock or soil by the action of wind, water, or ice.

Activity 1: Chill Out

1. Put the straw into the glass of water and suck until the straw is full.

2. Hold your tongue over the end of the straw and remove the straw from the water. The water should stay in the straw. Plug up the other end of the straw with a bit of clay or chewed chewing gum.

3. Move your tongue away and plug up that end with clay or chewing gum.

4. Place the straw in the freezer. Predict what you will see when the water in the straw freezes. Record your prediction and the reasons for it.

5. After a few hours, look at the straw in the freezer. Compare what has happened with what you predicted. Can you explain what happened? How does this relate to rocks?

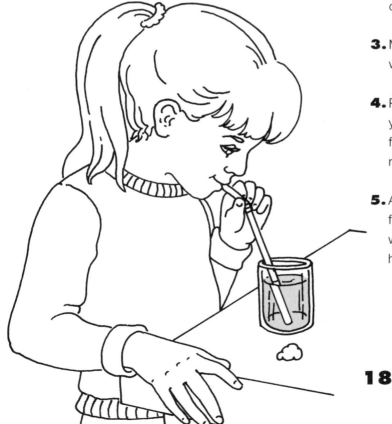

Activity 2: Drip, Drip, Drip

1. Weigh a new bar of soap on your scale.

2. Turn on a faucet so that it drips slowly.

3. Place the bar of soap beneath the drip. Let the water drip onto it overnight. Predict what will happen to the soap.

4. The next day, record a description of the soap. What is different? Has the weight changed? What do you think would happen if you left the soap under the faucet for a week? A month?

What does all this have to do with rocks?

Faking Fossils

YOU NEED:
activity 1 ★ Ten small, hard objects with distinctive shapes (for example, paper clip, pen, sea shell, key, spoon) ★ Modeling clay ★ Ten paper plates ★ A crayon or pencil

activity 2 ★ 4 oz (120 ml) white glue ★ Water ★ The last paper towel attached to its cardboard roll ★ A shallow pan that is longer than the paper towel roll ★ Plastic wrap

Have you ever sneaked cookies and even though no one saw you, your mom or dad knew you had done it? How did they know? You probably left some evidence behind—crumbs on the kitchen counter, perhaps, or a chocolaty thumbprint on the cookie jar.

In a similar way, plants and animals that lived many millions of years ago have left evidence of their existence in the form of fossil records. In fossils, you can see dinosaur tracks, imprints of entire animals or just their bones, and even, occasionally, the animals themselves, preserved just the way they looked so many years ago. Scientists use fossils to piece together stories of how ancient plants and animals lived.

On these pages you will find instructions for making your own fossils. While you're making them, think of what they could tell a future scientist about your life.

Activity 1: 20th-Century Fossils

1. Divide the clay into ten pieces and work with the pieces until they are soft and pliable. Set each piece on a separate paper plate.

2. Number the paper plates from 1 to 10. Write the number on the top of the plate, next to the clay.

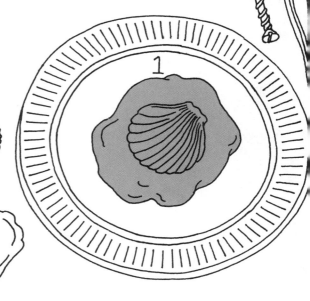

3. Press each of the distinctively shaped objects firmly into a piece of clay and then remove the objects. You should have a clear imprint of each object in the clay. On the back of the plate, identify the object.

4. Ask friends to guess which object made each imprint, without showing your friends the objects. Record their answers on a separate sheet of paper.

Activity 2: This Is Petrifying!

1. Combine the glue and the water in the bottom of the shallow pan to a depth of approximately 1/2 in (1.25 cm).

2. Place the paper towel and its roll in the mixture. Be sure you coat all surfaces.

3. Stand the roll on its end and let it dry. Keep the pan covered with plastic wrap while the roll dries.

4. When the roll and towel are dry, roll it in the glue/water mixture again. Repeat the process a total of four times.

5. Wait a week. While you wait, make a list of the qualities of a normal paper towel—for example, its color, weight, ability to absorb, and texture. Try to predict how the paper towel will have changed after the glue-and-water mixture has soaked into it and dried completely.

5. Evaluate how successful your friends were in recognizing the familiar objects. Which did they most easily identify? Which objects did they misidentify? Why?

6. Try the same experiment a second time. You could use the existing clay forms on different friends, or find other objects to imprint. Compare your results with those from your first experiment.

6. After a week, examine the paper towel and roll. What has changed? Compare the towel's qualities now with the ones you recorded earlier. In what specific ways is it different now?

7. Hypothesize the reasons for the changes.

Getting Clear on Crystals

YOU NEED:

activity 1 ★ A pipe cleaner ★ A glass ★ 4 oz (120 ml) hot water ★ Salt
★ A spoon ★ A pencil ★ A magnifying glass

activity 2 ★ 4 charcoal briquettes ★ A glass bowl ★ 1 Tbs (15 ml) household ammonia
★ 2 Tbs (30 ml) water ★ 1 Tbs (15 ml) noniodized salt ★ 2 Tbs (30 ml) laundry bluing
★ A medicine dropper ★ Food coloring ★ Safety glasses ★ A spoon ★ A magnifying glass

It has no nose, eyes, mouth or chin, yet it has a face. In fact, it often has many faces. What is it? It's a crystal, and its faces are its smooth, flat surfaces that meet each other at angles. Most of the nonliving material in the world is made of crystals.

An example of a crystal is a grain of salt. Take a good look at the shape of a grain of salt through a magnifying glass. Can you see its flat sides and sharp angles? Now look at a grain of sugar and compare it to the salt. How are they alike and how are they different? Which one has six sides, and which one has irregular sides? Are they both crystals? In the following activities, you will get a chance to make and examine your own crystals.

⚠ **Be extra careful when working with hot water.**

Activity 1: Growing Crystals

1. Bend the pipe cleaner into an interesting shape. Twist one end of the pipe cleaner onto the middle of a pencil.

2. Pour the hot water into the glass.

3. Put several spoonfuls of salt into the water. Stir after each spoonful. Stop when you see that the salt is not dissolving any more.

4. Lay the pencil across the top of the glass. Make sure that your pipe cleaner shape is dangling in the hot water.

5. Set the glass in a place where you know it will not be disturbed for several days.

6. Check the pipe cleaner after a few hours. You should see crystals growing on it.

7. After a few days, when the water is mostly gone, carefully slip the pipe cleaner off the pencil. Don't touch the crystals—they are very delicate.

8. Now you can look at the crystals with a magnifying glass. Try to see the flat surfaces and angles. If you like, you can hang up your crystal creation as a decoration. Record what happened to your crystals.

Activity 2: Crystal Garden

⚠ **For this activity, make sure you wear safety glasses and have a grown-up help you when handling the chemicals.**

1. Place the charcoal in the bowl.

2. Mix together the salt, ammonia, bluing, and water. Stir well.

3. Pour or spoon the mixture over the charcoal.

4. Drop a little food coloring on the charcoal. Let the charcoal sit undisturbed for about three days. What do you think will happen?

5. At the end of the three days, what do you see? What shapes do the crystals form? Examine them closely with a magnifying glass. Try to draw the crystals you see.

A **W**eather **S**tation for **C**louds and **R**ain

YOU NEED:
activity 1 ★ A sheet of clean paper ★ A mirror ★ A table or other flat surface
★ A compass ★ A marking pen

activity 2 ★ A soft drink bottle or other bottle made of plastic ★ Scissors or a knife
★ A ruler ★ A marking pen ★ A clear glass or jar about the same width across as
the funnel

You're lying on your back in the soft, green grass and what should float by? A turtle with two heads, a plate of scrambled eggs, a boat with wheels, and your Uncle Chester's nose. Are you dreaming? No, you're just looking up at the sky, letting your imagination make shapes of the clouds as they drift by.

When meteorologists look at clouds, they see more than imaginary shapes, though. Clouds help them predict the weather. So do the winds and the patterns of *precipitation* (prih SIHP uh TAY shun)—that is, rainfall and snowfall.

In the following pages, you'll discover ways you can observe and measure clouds, and the rainfall they sometimes bring.

Activity 1: They Went That-a-Way!

1. Place the paper on a table or other flat surface outside in an area free of tree branches and other obstructions.

2. Use a compass to identify north. Mark north, northeast, east, southeast, south, southwest, west, and northwest at the edges of your paper, using the marking pen.

3. Place the mirror in the center of the paper.

4. Look into the mirror to watch the clouds move across the sky. Record the direction that the clouds are coming from.

5. Try this experiment again on days when the weather is different. Again, record the direction the clouds are coming from. Did the direction change? Write down how you think the direction the clouds move is connected to the weather.

meteorologists
(mee tee uh ROL uh jihsts): scientists who study the weather.

Activity 2: Rain Gauge

1. Have a grown-up help you cut the top off the plastic bottle.

2. Place the top upside down in the glass or jar to make a funnel.

3. Using the ruler as a guide, draw marks at every half-inch on the side of the glass. You will use this scale to measure the rainfall.

4. Place the glass outside in an open area. You don't want water dripping off trees or roofs to spoil your data.

5. Make sure the bottle is firmly fixed in the ground, in case a strong wind comes. On a chart, predict how much rain will fill the jar the next few times it rains.

6. Wait until it rains.

7. Check the rain gauge after each rain. On your chart, record the amount of rain that fell each day, along with the date. Be sure to empty the glass each day after you have recorded the water level.

You may want to listen to the weather report daily to see if your rain gauge recorded the same amount of rain as the official rain gauge. If your report is different, try to figure out reasons why.

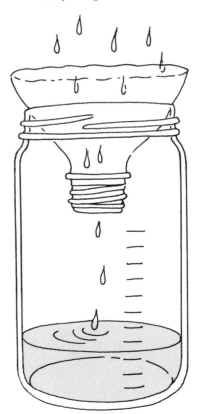

A Weather Station for Wind

YOU NEED:
- ★ A paper cup ★ A drinking straw ★ Modeling clay ★ A pencil with eraser
- ★ A straight pin ★ Scissors ★ Flat board made of wood or heavy cardboard
- ★ Thin cardboard ★ A compass ★ A pen, pencil, or marker

Wind is a major factor in our weather. Wind is caused when air masses flow from an area of high pressure to one of low pressure. When the wind starts to blow, you can be sure that a change of weather is on the way. The change may be small, or it may warn you to prepare for a wild, windy day or night.

A well-known device for finding out the direction the wind is coming from is the weather vane. People have been using weather vanes for centuries to see which way the wind blows. People in the Northern Hemisphere know that *northerly winds* (that is, from the north) often bring cool, dry weather and that *southerly winds* usually bring warm, wet weather. This is your chance to make your own weather vane and to discover how the direction of the wind affects your weather.

1. Make a hole in the center of the paper cup bottom. Working from the bottom of the cup, push the pencil, point down, into the hole.

2. Affix modeling clay along the brim of the paper cup. Then set the cup, brim down, onto the board. (The clay will keep the weather vane from getting blown away.)

3. Cut two isosceles triangles from the thin cardboard. See the picture for the correct sizes. Make sure one is bigger than the other.

isosceles (eye SAHS uh leez): having two equal sides.

4. Cut a slit in each end of the drinking straw. Slip the two cardboard triangles into the slits. (See the picture.) You might want to use some glue, too.

5. Push the pin through the middle of the straw and then into the top of the pencil eraser. Don't smash the straw. It should move freely.

6. Set the weather vane down outside. Use a compass to find out which way is north and then mark all the directions on the board.

7. When the wind blows, the straw should move around. The triangles will point in the direction the wind is coming from.

8. Keep a record of the wind direction and the weather for a few weeks. How does the wind direction affect your weather? Draw a picture or write a story of your observations.

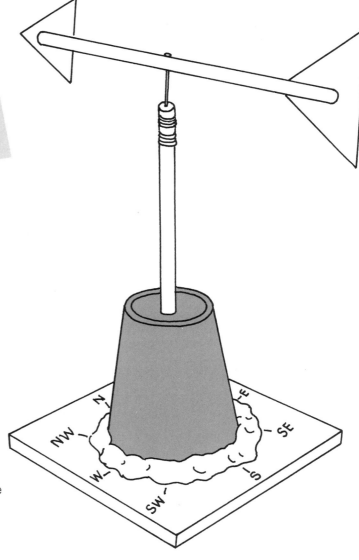

Rain Pellets

YOU NEED:
★ A pie tin ★ A clear plastic ruler ★ A fine-mesh wire strainer or a flour sifter ★ A bag of flour
★ A magnifying glass ★ Paper or newspaper ★ A spray can of shellac ★ A rainy day

Raindrops are raindrops. They're all the same, right? Wrong. Raindrops vary in size like just about everything in nature. Here is a method for taking a really good look at the size of a raindrop.

⚠ **Get a grown-up's permission before you use the kitchen supplies and have him or her help you use the oven and the shellac. DO NOT perform this activity when there is lightning outside.**

1. Pour a 1-in (2.5-cm) layer of flour on the bottom of the pie tin.

2. Go outside during a good, steady rain and let about 20 raindrops fall into the flour layer. Don't let the flour get too wet, or it will become pasty.

3. Go back inside. Gently pour the flour through the sifter. Each pellet that remains in the sifter has been created by a raindrop.

4. Examine the pellets. Record the answers to these questions or your own: How big is the biggest one and the smallest one? What is the average size of the pellets? Sort the pellets from smallest to largest.

5. To keep your pellets for further study, you can bake them. Just carefully place them on a cookie sheet or clean pie tin. Bake them for 5 or 10 minutes in an oven set at a medium temperature. When they are cool, put them on paper and spray them with shellac.

6. Try the experiment again in different kinds of rains. In your notebook, predict what will happen and then compare the results with your predictions. Are the pellets larger or smaller in heavy storms? Are they larger or smaller in drizzles? Are they different shapes? Try to think of reasons for the differences.

Twister in a Bottle

YOU NEED
★ Two large, plastic soda or water bottles of the same size ★ Waterproof tape
★ Confetti, paper punches, or any small bits of paper ★ Water

A tornado is the most violent type of storm there is. Its winds can whirl at speeds of more than 200 miles (320 kilometers) per hour and tear up trees by their roots, fling cars around like toys, and flatten buildings. A tornado forms when rotating air at the bottom of a dense, dark thundercloud descends toward the ground. You can make a model of a tornado in a bottle to observe how its winds swirl.

1. Put a few pinches of paper bits into one of the bottles.

2. Fill the same bottle about two-thirds full of water.

3. Match up the mouths of the bottles as shown and tape them together tightly so that no water will leak out.

4. Flip the bottles over so that the water is in the top bottle. At the same time, start moving the top bottle in a circle so that the water swirls around rapidly.

5. Stop moving the bottle and watch the water form a tornado shape as it flows into the bottom bottle. The paper bits will make the "tornado" easier to see.

Eyes on the Skies

YOU NEED:
★ A glass of water ★ A flashlight ★ Whole milk ★ An eyedropper ★ A spoon

Night is black, day is blue. It seems obvious. But have you ever wondered why? During daytime hours, when our side of the planet Earth faces the sun, the sky is light. But during the night, when our side faces away from the sun, the sky is dark. When it's light, why is it blue rather than another color? Try the following activity and find out.

1. Place the clear glass filled with water at eye level in a darkened room.

2. Shine the flashlight at the glass of water. The beam of light should go through the center of the water.

3. Record what you see. Does the beam of light pass through the water easily?

4. Now, using the eyedropper, place one drop of milk into the water. Stir the milk into the water with the spoon.

5. Take a moment to think about what may happen when you shine the light into the water. Record your prediction.

6. Now shine the flashlight into the water again. This time, what do you see? What do you think is causing the different color? How might the glass of milky water be like the sky? Record your observations and your explanation of what is happening.

Tabletop Telescope

YOU NEED:
★ A flat mirror ★ A magnifying mirror (the kind adults use to shave or put on makeup)
★ A magnifying glass ★ A table ★ A clear night sky with the moon (and maybe some stars) visible

From huge reflectors 1,000 feet (300 meters) wide to tiny binoculars you can fit in your pocket, most telescopes work in basically the same way—they collect and focus light in order to bring distant objects close-up. You can look at the night sky with a simple telescope you make yourself. Here's how:

1. Place the magnifying mirror near a window to reflect the moon or stars. Adjust the mirror so that it stands at an angle to the window so that the reflected light is visible against the window or the wall next to it.

2. Prop up the flat mirror between the magnifying mirror and the window or wall, in the path of the reflected light. From behind the magnifying mirror, you should see its reflection in the flat mirror. You may need to adjust the position and angle of both mirrors to get a good reflection of the moon or a group of stars. After every few minutes, you will have to readjust the mirrors because of the motion of the moon and stars.

3. Use your magnifying glass to examine the reflection that appears in the flat mirror. Move the magnifying glass back and forth until you see the reflection clearly. How well your telescope works depends on the quality of your magnifying glass and on finding the right distance and angles between the mirrors.

Answer **K**ey

Up and Down and Side to Side
Pages 12-13

Activity 1: Rooting Roots

Geotropism is the tendency of certain parts of plants to grow in a certain direction in response to the pull of gravity. Roots grow toward the source of gravity (Earth), and stems grow away from the source of gravity.

Activity 2: Plant Workout

Phototropism is the tendency of plants to grow in a certain direction in response to light. Most plants grow toward light. Your plant grows in a zig-zag pattern as it bends to where the light comes through the cards.

How Does Your Tongue Taste?
Pages 14-15

The back of the tongue is sensitive to bitter tastes, the front to sweets, and the edges, or sides, to salty and sour tastes.

You've Got Some Nerve(s)!
Pages 16-17

Activity 1: Finding Your Blind Spot

Normally we don't notice the blind spot because our eyes make so many quick movements. Also, whatever is in the blind spot of one eye can be seen by the other eye.

Do-It-Yourself Erosion
Pages 18-19

Activity 1: Chill Out

The water pushed the clay plug out of the straw because when water freezes, it expands. When the weather is cold, water in cracks of rocks freezes. The pressure of the frozen water can move or break the rocks.

Activity 2: Drip, Drip, Drip

The dripping water caused the soap to *erode,* or wear away, in one small spot. Water that falls on rocks erodes them in the same way.

Faking Fossils
Pages 20-21

Activity 2: This Is Petrifying!

The glue and water solution seeped into the air pockets of the absorbent paper towel and cardboard roll. In doing so, it changed the composition of the towel, making it harder and less absorbent. A similar process took place in many fossils long ago. Then, a mineral such as silica seeped into the pores in plant and animal life. It made a harder substance that retained the shapes of the original living things.

A Weather Station for Clouds and Rain
Pages 24-25

Activity 1: They Went That-a-Way!

New weather systems are usually blown in with the wind. Clouds high in the atmosphere are not interrupted by big buildings or trees. So the clouds blown by these winds are good indicators of the direction of winds that are affecting an area.

Eyes on the Skies
Page 30

The water should be a pale gray-blue. White light is made of different waves of color, and the waves are different sizes. When the light from the flashlight hits the tiny particles of milk mixed with the water, blue waves within the white light are separated and spread through the water, causing the water to look bluish. In the sky, nitrogen and oxygen molecules also separate blue light waves from the white sunlight, making the sky look blue.